The Dolls' House Book

The Dolls' House Book

PAULINE FLICK

Collins St James's Place London

William Collins Sons & Co Ltd
London · Glasgow · Sydney · Auckland
Toronto · Johannesburg

400013408

J 745. 59 FLI
J099377

First published 1973
© Pauline Flick 1973
ISBN 0 00 192156 8
Made and Printed in Great Britain by
William Collins Sons & Co Ltd Glasgow

Acknowledgments

I am most grateful to the following for allowing me to use their photographs:

Hawkley Studio Associates Ltd. (Front and back cover, frontispiece, and opposite pages 16, 32, 80, 81, 112). Mr Gordon Wells (opposite page 113). The London Museum (opposite pages 33, 64, 65). City of Manchester Art Galleries (opposite page 17). Stockport Museum (opposite page 96).

The drawings on pages 48 and 49 are by Ian Douglass, and are reproduced by kind permission of Messrs Whitmore Gwillim & Company; those on pages 78, 79, 81 and 89 are by Bertha Stamp, reproduced by courtesy of Routledge & Kegan Paul Ltd. The illustrations on pages 32 and 46 are from the Mary Evans Picture Library. I should also like to thank Enid Fairhead for all her help and patience over the design of this book.

The
History of
Dolls' Houses

The History
of Dolls' Houses

There's something mysterious about a dolls' house. If you already have one of your own, you'll know how a strange, secret life seems to be going on inside the tiny rooms; most people would like to be small enough – just sometimes – to walk in through the front door and make themselves at home, joining the dolls in their silent, cluttered little world.

This is what often happens in stories – think of *Gulliver* and *Alice in Wonderland* and *The Borrowers* – but never, unfortunately, in ordinary nurseries. So the next best thing is to look in from the outside, pick up the minute pieces of furniture, the stiff dolls and the bright plates of plaster food, and try changing them about, adding perhaps a picture here and a new bedcover there. It's odd that we should enjoy this dolls' 'housework' so much, when in real life bed-making and table-laying are so tedious. It must, I think, be because of the in-

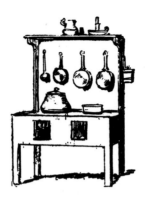

credible *smallness* of everything: there's a magic about even the dullest object if only it's tiny enough. For instance, take an everyday kitchen saucepan – nobody would give it a second glance. But pick up a *toy* saucepan no bigger than an acorn cup and you know straight away that you are holding something special.

I had a lovely old Victorian dolls' house in my nursery, and used to play with it for hours. The furniture was always being moved from one room to another, and new curtains and carpets cut out from scraps of material. After all, there's a lot to be said for being able to whisk a grand piano upstairs in less than a minute, or re-decorate a whole room with only a yard of left-over wallpaper – you do get quick results. When I grew up I began to hunt round for more dolls' houses and miniature pieces of furniture, and before I knew what was happening I'd become a 'Collector'. Now I'm always looking in toyshops and antique markets and jumble sales to see what I can find, and trying to discover more about these fascinating old toys by going to see the ones on show in various museums. Their history goes back for hundreds of years, and in some families a beautiful dolls' house has been passed down as an heirloom from generation to generation. These valuable houses were often designed by architects and built by clever cabinet-makers, but there are many others which were obviously put together at home by loving fathers, or even by the children themselves. The furniture might be anything from an exquisite miniature chest of drawers to a home-made bed which is just a cardboard box and its lid fitted together and draped with muslin. The earliest dolls' house families were made of wax or wood; in Victorian times they usually had china heads, and came from Germany; after that they were made of celluloid, and now they are nearly all plastic. The amazing thing is that so many of the very old dolls, and their wonderful doll-mansions, are still as good as new, and we can go and admire them in museums. In this book I have tried to describe several dolls' houses of different dates to show how they have gradually changed over the centuries. Though really, when you come to think about it, in many ways they have hardly changed at all . . . the most important thing, the wonderful *smallness*, is always the same.

Nearly three hundred years ago a little girl named Ann Sharp had a dolls' house. She was one of the first English children to have a toy like this, as the craze for miniature houses had only just reached this country from Germany and Holland. Although Ann was born so long ago, in 1691 to be exact, we know quite a lot about her: her father was the Archbishop of York, she had thirteen brothers and sisters, and one of her godmothers was the Royal Princess who later became Queen Anne. It was this Royal godmother who gave little Ann the dolls' house, and the most surprising thing about this wonderful present is that it still exists. If you are ever in Norwich, go to the Strangers' Hall Museum and you can see it, looking almost exactly as it did when Ann and her brothers and sisters played with it in York.

The first thing you notice is its enormous size, for it is nearly six feet high and has nine rooms. There must have been great excitement when it was delivered to the Archbishop's Palace – perhaps it was a surprise for Ann Sharp's birthday one year – and it is easy to imagine the children climbing onto chairs and tables to peer into the upstairs rooms. What they saw was better than anything they could ever have dreamed of: the house was filled with wax dolls in sumptuous dresses, fourposter beds with damask curtains, real silver candlesticks, tiny ivory boxes, tables, chairs, a cooked chicken on a dish, pewter plates, kitchen scales, a baby in a cradle – wherever they looked they saw a new treasure. The younger children must have longed to take the tiny things out and examine them, but evidently Ann and her mother were very strict: the dolls' house was always treated with the greatest care, and nothing was ever allowed to get lost or broken.

Even today the dolls still have the labels which Ann pinned to their clothes, showing the name she gave each one. The head of the household is labelled 'My Lord Rochett', and in keeping with his high position he is grandly dressed in pink and silver satin, and wears a powdered wig. Besides his wife, Lady Rochett, and a son called William there are various servants – 'Fanny Long, ye Chamber-maid', 'Roger ye Butler', 'Sarah Gill, child's maid', and 'Mrs. Hannah, ye housekeeper'. Then there are some guests who have come to dinner, a little girl in a wide-skirted yellow dress, and of course the pale waxy baby lying in its cradle.

The words 'dolls' house' didn't come into use until the beginning of the nineteenth century, and the little Sharps would have called Ann's lovely toy a 'baby-house'. Apart from the baby-house they would have had very few things to play with, simply because hardly any toys were made in those days. Probably the girls had one or two larger wooden dolls with painted pink cheeks and dark glass eyes, all dressed as grown-up ladies in silk gowns, quilted petticoats and fine knitted stockings.

The little boys might have had a rocking horse – just a roughly carved head on solid rockers – and some hoops, balls and marbles. But children at the beginning of the eighteenth century had very little time for play, and were expected to spend most of the day at their lessons and generally getting ready to take their place in the grown-up world as soon as possible. There were no children's story books – because none had been written yet – and apart from lesson books there was nothing for them to read but rather frightening religious works and manuals on good behaviour. Even their clothes were copies of grown-up fashions – tight breeches for little boys and hooped skirts for girls. Romping and jumping about were strongly disapproved of, but dancing, riding, needlework and anything else which would be useful in later life were encouraged.

Even Ann's baby-house wasn't meant to be just a toy. As well as being something to play with, it was a help in teaching her how to run a household – how to organise servants, arrange furniture in various rooms, dust, polish and, most important of all, how to use all the pots and pans in the kitchen.

When she was twenty-one Ann married a clergyman, and went to live in Ripon. But she kept her baby-house, and in due course it was passed on to her eldest son John and his family. They added a few extras like the dear little china dinner service, the silver teapot and the toy theatre, which is made of paper and is complete with scenery and actors. When we think how many children must have played with the baby-house, and how fragile the furniture is – how easy, for instance, to step accidentally on a minute dining chair, or to drop a pair of fire tongs through a crack in the nursery floor – it is all the more amazing that there is so much left. The only important thing to have got lost is the front of the house, which disappeared many years ago. It seems, though, that it only looked like an ordinary cupboard door, and not the outside of a real house, so the loss is not too serious.

It was quite usual for some early dolls' houses to look like cupboards when they were closed, although others were made with wonderful fronts designed by real architects, with sliding sash windows, chimneys, flights of steps and doors with handles and knockers. There is a baby-house in the Castle Museum at York which was originally made for the family at nearby Heslington Hall just a year or two after Ann Sharp's, and its front is just like that of a real house. Possibly it was designed by the famous architect Sir John Vanbrugh, when he wasn't too busy writing plays or drawing up the plans for full-size mansions like Blenheim Palace or Castle Howard.

A little later, about 1730, an even more wonderful baby-house was made for a child called Sarah Lethieullier. Her family had come to England from Belgium, which explains her foreign-sounding name, and when she grew up she married an Englishman, Sir Matthew Fetherstonhaugh. Sarah took the baby-house with her to her new home at Uppark, in Sussex, and after more than two hundred years it is still there today, as perfect as ever. It is three storeys high, with twenty windows, classical pillars and seven graceful statues lined up along the roof. Many baby-houses of this period had special stands made for them, so they looked more like important pieces of furniture than children's toys. The stand for Sarah's house was very cleverly designed to represent stables and a coach-house, and although the toy horses and carriages have unfortunately been lost, the stand itself, with its arched openings and carved 'stone-work', is still there with the baby-house. Sarah kept her beautiful toy on the landing at the top of the stairs, and although she was now Lady Fetherstonhaugh and quite grown-up, she still enjoyed rearranging the furniture and adding new pieces from time to time. Like Ann Sharp's, Sarah's house was most carefully looked after, and almost everything is still exactly as it was when she used to play with it.

It has four-poster beds with silk curtains, a cradle

The Dolls' House at Nostell Priory, in Yorkshire (page 19)

"Domestic Happiness" by George Morland, engraved by William Ward.
Note the small dolls' house on the floor (page 23).

with twin babies lying in it, chandeliers, oil paintings, silver teaspoons, a mousetrap and dozens of other delights. Many of these tiny objects tell us a lot about life in a full-size house of that time, as the dolls' house rooms have never been altered and brought up to date as rooms in real houses have been. For instance, it is very rare to find a full-size house still lit by lamps and candles, but these are very common in dolls' houses, along with tinder boxes and snuffers and all the other equipment that used to be needed for lighting. It is difficult now to imagine how people managed without electricity or gas, but a baby-house like Sarah's shows how beds were warmed with brass warming pans filled with hot cinders – there were no hot water bottles, let alone electric blankets – and ironing had to be done with an iron heated by a hot brick. Most meat was cooked in front of an open fire, and these old dolls' houses often have miniature spits for turning a joint, racks for warming plates and other strange kitchen utensils. I've even heard of a baby-house with chicken coops in the kitchen, so that poultry could be fattened up on scraps and then killed and eaten when needed; at first it sounds rather cruel, as the poor hens probably imagined they were household pets, but on the other hand it must have been a most convenient arrangement before refrigerators and deep freezers were invented.

Sarah was certainly not the only grown-up who enjoyed playing with baby-houses. In the first half of the eighteenth century these 'toys' were just as popular, if not more so, with adults as they were with children, and the really valuable ones would never have been kept in the nursery. Usually they stood either in the drawing room or on the landing, with their fronts securely locked, and children would have been allowed to touch them only when a grown-up was there to see that the delicate furnishings came to no harm. Even so, these English houses, no matter how grand, were more toy-like than the early German and Dutch models had been, and always look as if they were meant to be played with by *somebody*.

A Yorkshire Baby-House

One reason why baby-houses were so popular in this country was that everyone in the eighteenth century was tremendously interested in architecture, and hundreds of elegant mansions sprang up all over England. Everybody wanted a house in the fashionable 'classical' style, with a flat front and tall sash windows spaced out evenly on either side of the entrance door. Many of the grander houses, especially those standing in country parks, had pillars and a pediment, like a Greek or Roman temple. The door and window frames were nearly always painted white, which looked very smart against the neat red bricks or smooth stone of the walls.

Besides being such a good style for a real house, this new way of building was ideal for the baby-house maker to copy: the flat front made a convenient door which could be opened in one piece, showing all the rooms inside, and carpenters employed on the great estates up and down the country set to work to make model houses for children and grown-ups to play with.

In about 1740 two sisters called Lady Winn and Miss Henshaw had the idea of making a baby-house in the same style as their own home, which was itself being rebuilt to bring it up to date, and was only half-finished at the time. The full-size house was Nostell Priory, near Wakefield, which is now looked after by the National Trust, and the baby-house is still there too, well over two hundred years old.

The sisters evidently spent an enormous amount of time and trouble on the design of their lovely toy. Probably they had some help from the architect of Nostell Priory itself, for the baby-house with its imposing portico has something of the same look as the mansion. The tiny pieces of furniture are so beautifully made they almost take one's breath away: there is a grandfather clock, an exquisite walnut bureau and a canopied State Bed; Chinese wallpaper, covered with birds and flowers; locks and handles (which work) on the doors, marble chimney-pieces, and a family of dolls too, of course, made of wax and dressed in the most magnificent clothes.

Nostell Priory is now open to the public, and if you are ever in that part of Yorkshire do try to go there and see the baby-house, still in the same perfect condition as the day it was made.

Baby-Houses Move into the Nursery

If you live near London, or come on a visit sometime, the best place to see old dolls' houses is the Bethnal Green Museum (very easy to get to by the Underground). There are always about a dozen houses on show, as well as miniature kitchens, model shops and a feast of other old toys. The most impressive dolls' house there is the Tate Baby-House, made in Dorset in 1760, which has beautiful curving steps leading up to the front door and an elegant balustrade round the roof. Nothing definite is known about the Tate children who first played with it, but we can be fairly sure they were allowed to have more fun with it than the little Sharps had with Ann's baby-house sixty years earlier. Nursery life had suddenly become much brighter in the middle of the eighteenth century, and although an outstanding model like the Tate house would probably still have been kept in the drawing room, plenty of less elaborate baby-houses were made for ordinary play. It was at this time that all sorts of new ideas on how families should be brought up and educated came into fashion, and parents began to realise that a certain amount of

Of course it is the grand, valuable baby-houses which have survived from the eighteenth century, and can still be seen in museums. But we know quite a lot about the more ordinary ones from artists and writers of the time, and from the trade catalogues sent out by the German toy merchants. George Morland, the famous English artist, painted a picture called 'Domestic Happiness' in about 1780 which shows a little 'one up and one down' dolls house quite casually lying on the floor. At about the same time a lady poet called Adelaide O'Keefe wrote these verses about a dolls' house; notice, though, that she still calls it a 'baby-house'.

A NEW YEAR'S GIFT

A charming present comes from town,
    A baby-house so neat;
With kitchen, parlour, dining room,
    And chambers all complete.

A gift to Emma and to Rose,
    From grandpapa it came;
The little Rosa smiled delight
    And Emma did the same.

They eagerly examined all:
    The furniture was gay;
And in the rooms they placed their dolls,
    When dressed in fine array.

At night, their little family
    Must tenderly be fed;
And then, when dollies were undressed,
    They all were put to bed.

Thus Rose and Emma passed each hour,
    Devoted to their play;
And long were cheerful, happy, kind –
    Nor cross disputes had they.

Till Rose in baby-house would change
    The chairs which were below:
'This carpet they would better suit;
    I think I'll have it so.'

'No, no, indeed,' her sister said,
    'I'm older, Rose, than you;
And I'm the mistress, you the maid,
    And what I bid must do.'

The quarrel grew to such a height,
    Mamma she heard the noise,
And coming in, beheld the floor
    All strewn with broken toys.

'Oh, fie, my Emma! fie, my Rose!
    Say, what is this about?
Remember, this is New-year's day,
    And both are going out.'

Now Betty calls the little girls
    To come up-stairs and dress;
They still dispute, with muttered taunts,
    And anger they express.

But just prepared to leave their room,
    Persisting yet in strife,
Rose sickening fell on Betty's lap,
    As if devoid of life.

Mamma appeared at Betty's call –
   John for the doctor goes;
And some disease of dangerous kind,
   Its symptoms soon disclose.

'But though I stay, my Emma, you
   May go and spend the day.'
'Oh no, mamma,' replied the child,
   I must with Rosa stay.

'Beside my sister's bed I'll sit,
   And watch her with such care:
No pleasure can I e'er enjoy,
   Till she my pleasure share.

'How silly now seems our dispute; –
   Not one of us she knows!
How pale she looks, how hard she breathes!
   Alas! my pretty Rose!'

Children in stories and poems of this period are
often made to behave in this most unnatural way.
Miss O'Keefe doesn't actually say so, but I should
think Rose probably died and Emma was taught a
smart lesson against quarrelling and bad temper.
Although life in the nursery was much more
carefree than it had been, writers still felt they
should do all they could to encourage good behaviour by pointing out the awful consequences of
behaving badly. Still, anybody interested in early
dolls' houses must be grateful to Miss O'Keefe for
her description of little girls actually playing with
one and breaking things.

Dolls' Houses by the Thousand

The nineteenth century was the time when by far
the most dolls' houses of all sorts and sizes were
produced, and no nursery was complete without
one. Queen Victoria had one when she was a child,

and it is still kept in the State Apartments at Kensington Palace. It is very plain, just two rooms – one up and one down – and it has lost most of its furniture. But over a hundred wooden dolls which the little Princess Victoria dressed (with quite a lot of help from her governess, as she herself admitted) and which would have been about the right size for the house, have all survived, and are displayed separately.

By this time most dolls' house furniture was imported from Germany, where it was made in vast quantities and great variety. Manufacturers published lovely coloured catalogues illustrating all the different things they could supply, and luckily some of these, as well as lots of the furniture itself, can still be seen. It didn't matter how big or small a dolls' house was, the right size of firegrate, clock, washstand, sewing table and birdcage could all be bought for it, as well as the more ordinary necessities of life like dining-room tables, chairs, sofas, pianos and beds. I have seen a catalogue dated 1836 which even included tiny stags' heads, mounted on wooden shields, to hang up in the dolls' house hall – a very baronial touch. They look so nice that I have

invented a way of copying them for home-made houses, and you will see how to do this in the second part of this book.

Nearly all the dolls' houses displayed in museums are labelled 'Victorian', but as the Queen reigned from 1837 to 1901 this description covers a great many years and changes of style, from flat-fronted classical mansions like the eighteenth century baby-houses to the gabled suburban villas of the 1890s. Probably there is at least one on show in your local museum, and even if there isn't it's worth asking if there is one put away somewhere out of sight; often museums don't have enough space to put every-thing out at once, but the curator will usually let you have a look at things in store if you ask specially. At the end of this section I have made out a list of places where some of the best dolls' houses are kept; if you can manage to visit one or two of them you will soon see how perfectly these old toys sum up the Victorian way of life – dark rooms with thick curtains and carpets, heavy furniture, masses of ornaments, dozens of servants and *mountains* of food.

unheard of. Besides doing embroidery and patchwork, making pictures out of seaweed and shells,
playing the piano and filling albums with family
portraits, they often helped children make things
for their dolls' houses. They sewed tiny clothes for

[1] Home-made chairs
Cardboard sections are oversewn together. The
legs of the armchair can be made from beads
threaded onto pins.

the inhabitants, stitched away at miniature petit-
point carpets and painstakingly cut out paper
furniture from the printed sheets then sold in
toyshops. Upholstered sofas and chairs, made at
home from cardboard sections covered with
material and then oversewn together, can still be
found in many old dolls' houses *[1]*.

They are not at all difficult to copy, and you can
finish them off with rows of pins to look like
upholstery nails, as Victorian children did. Sets of
furniture made from feathers, although they sound

so frail, still survive and are on show in several museums. Only the strong feathers from a bird's tail and wings were used, and they were carefully trimmed so that the bare quill formed the chair legs while four flat feathery bits were cleverly overlapped to look just like a rush seat. It must have taken a lot of skill and patience, but any child, however clumsy, could manage to make 'conker' furniture; this only needed large horse-chestnuts, some long steel pins and odd lengths of wool or silk thread. For a chair you stuck four pins into a flattish conker for the legs, then added four more to make the back support, which was filled in by weaving thread in and out of the pins [2].

When the Victorians had goose for dinner, which was fairly often, especially around St Michael's

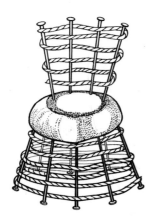

[2] A conker chair
It can either have four plain pin legs, or a woven base to match the back. Try using raffia for a 'wicker' effect.

[3] A goose wishbone chair

Day, 29 September, and at Christmas time, the bird's curved wish-bone would be saved to make a little three-cornered arm-chair: the bone provided the arms and front legs (all in one piece), so that the only other things needed were a short stick for the single back leg and a triangle of cardboard for the seat, which was usually covered with velvet and then glued into place. Anyone who has goose for Christmas dinner could easily copy this idea (but be sure to give the wish-bone a good scrub first) *[3]*.

In 1860 'The Girls' Own Toymaker and Book of Recreation' was published, and this gave instructions for making more dolls' house furniture. Some of the suggestions are terribly complicated and difficult to follow, and many little girls must have wept bitterly as their flimsy paper houses collapsed in sticky heaps. A child was expected to be able to produce a 'rustic Swiss Cottage' covered with little twigs carefully split in two, a three-wheeled paper perambulator, a half-tester bed, a couch and a washstand, all from the scantiest of diagrams. On the next two pages there are simpler patterns for making Victorian dolls' furniture out of paper or cardboard.

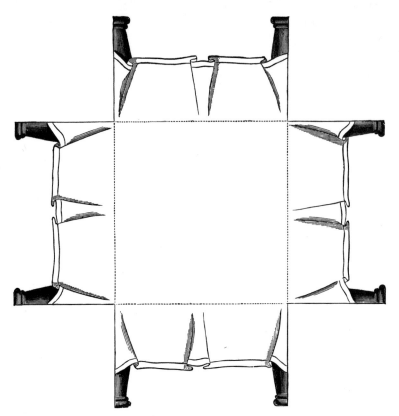

Table with Tablecloth

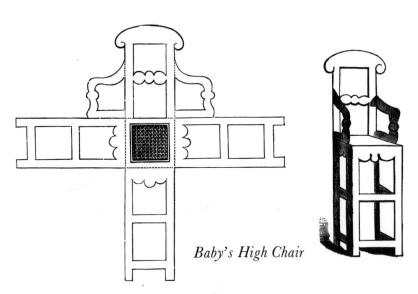

Baby's High Chair

Bureau

At least two of the Girls' Own Toymaker patterns below are quick and easy to copy – the ones for a fireplace and a fender. I have tried them both, using stiff black paper for the grate and yellow, to look like brass, for the fender, and they have turned out very well. So if you want to go back a hundred and ten years, and try your hand at a real Victorian pastime, here are the diagrams and the words of instruction just as they appear in the book:

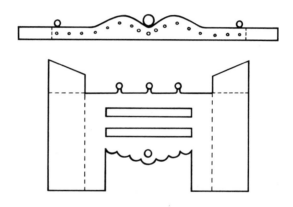

[4] Grate and Fender from 'The Girls' Own Toymaker' published in 1860
Cut out the form of this figure, perforate the holes with the point of a pin, and bend over the ends from the dotted lines to form the fender.

The dolls' houses made during the last few years of the nineteenth century were often not quite so well finished off as the earlier ones had been – the rooms sometimes had no doors, and the staircases no banisters. But even so they were still very grand and imposing, with a great many rooms. Nurseries were large and there was plenty of space for big toys, not to mention strict nannies to make sure they were carefully looked after. A very fine dolls' house made about 1890 is now on view in Northumberland; it has been given to the National Trust and taken to Wallington Hall, a stately home about twenty miles north of Newcastle-upon-Tyne. This dolls' mansion – for it is far more than a mere *house* – is over nine feet long and has thirty-six rooms, all with their original wallpapers and carpets or linoleum. It is furnished with nearly a thousand different pieces of dolls' house furniture and fifty little dolls dressed to represent the family and their servants. There is even a lift which really works, and running water supplied from a tank on the roof; it must have been greatest fun to play with.

For the first few years of the twentieth century life went on much as it had in the nineteenth. But gradually fewer people built themselves enormous houses, and as a result there were fewer enormous dolls' houses. In 'The Tale of Two Bad Mice' Beatrix Potter wrote about the sort of dolls' house being made at this time, and if you have ever read it you will remember the adorable pictures she drew to go with her story. The drawings are quite clearly based on a house which she knew well, and the book is dedicated to 'the little girl who had the dolls' house'. It is the sort of house you might find anywhere, red brick with a green front door and muslin curtains, but even so the *smallness* of everything makes it special. The furniture is the right size for mice, and all the well-known dolls' house pieces are there – a birdcage, a kitchen grate filled with a 'red-hot crinkly paper fire', a plaster ham glued to its dish, fire-irons, and a wicker cradle which Hunca Munca drags off for her own mouse-babies.

The catalogues sent out by big London shops show the kind of dolls' houses on sale in their toy departments at this time. In 1907 The Army and Navy Stores stocked both English-made and foreign dolls' houses, varying in price from 10/6 (about 50p) to 70/– (£3·50). For well under £2·00 you could buy a nice little four-roomed house with a porch and a bay window with lace curtains. A box

of dolls' house furniture costs less than 5p, but anything as cheap as this was probably made of cardboard printed with pretty colours. Metal furniture was very cheap too – a coal-scuttle or a dear little high-chair cost one (old) penny. By now almost all dolls' houses and their furnishings were mass-produced in factories, and although they weren't as magnificent as the earlier hand-made ones had been they were still very popular and every little girl wanted one.

Most children were quite content with something quite small, but one little girl who lived in Ireland had a wonderful fairy palace made for her. Her name was Guendoline, and her father, Sir Nevile Wilkinson, spent fifteen years organising the building of the palace and collecting miniature treasures to furnish it with. By the time he had finished it was nothing like an ordinary toy dolls' house, but was a perfect model of a grand Italian *palazzo*, with inlaid floors, mosaic ceilings and carved chimney-pieces. The various rooms are arranged round a flower-filled courtyard, and the family who is supposed to inhabit this magnificent dwelling consists of Titania, the fairy queen, her husband Oberon, and their children the fairy princesses. Like all true fairies, though, they are absolutely invisible; only the tiny possessions they have left lying about show that they live there. The princesses have minute tooth-brushes, and Oberon has a minuscule collar-stud on his dressing-table. There are tiny books and newspapers in the library, and a jewelled throne for Titania in the royal presence-chamber. There is even an organ that can be played by having its keys pressed down with matchsticks, and windows with stained glass panes. Of course Guendoline was grown up before this lovely house was completed, and instead of being kept at home for her to play with it was sent to London, where it was put on view to raise money for children's charities. Afterwards it went all round the world, collecting more money, and came back with several more treasures picked up on its travels – a tiny enamel horse, three thousand years old, made by the Ancient Egyptians, a green malachite kiwi from New Zealand, and a gold beaver from Canada.

*　　*　　*

Queen Mary's Dolls' House at Windsor Castle is another model that was never meant to be a nursery toy. It was presented to Queen Mary in 1924, after a group of artists and craftsmen had had the idea of making a miniature mansion furnished with everything one might expect to find in a royal palace at that time. Each tiny piece of furniture was made to an exact scale by skilled cabinet makers, and the building itself was designed by the celebrated architect Sir Edwin Lutyens. If you ever go to Windsor Castle and see it, you will get a wonderful picture of just how life was lived in a great house in the 1920s: there are damask table-cloths (specially woven, of course), leather despatch boxes in the study, awaiting the Monarch's attention, and dignified Rolls-Royce cars in the garage. The amount of detail is almost unbelievable: tiny jars hold real jam, the best wines are laid down in minute quantities in the cellar, and the pictures on the walls are paintings by well-known artists of the day. A gramophone record of the National Anthem, exactly the right size for the house, can really be played. The firm that made this record specially for Queen Mary's Dolls' House did in fact turn out quite a number of identical ones, and they were sold to the public as souvenirs; that was nearly fifty years ago, but several of them seem to have survived and collectors are always on the look-out for them.

Both Queen Mary's Dolls' House and Titania's Palace are far more like the very first grown-up baby-houses – the ones made in Germany and Holland and intended to display valuable minia-tures – than our idea of a dolls' house. Each room is already so perfectly arranged that it is quite impossible to think of trying out the furniture in different positions, and, still more important, there aren't any dolls to give the houses a 'toy-like' look and bring them to life. A dolls' house for playing with must have a family living in it – just think of all the fun Ann Sharp had labelling the inhabitants of her baby-house and making up stories about them all.

A writer called M. R. James even made up a ghost story about a family of dolls'-house dolls. He wrote it specially for the Library of Queen Mary's dolls' house, but it is all about a very old house, much older and quite different from the Queen's. His haunted dolls' house has pointed gothic windows, turrets, pinnacles and buttresses, a bell tower, and a chapel with stained glass windows. The doll population consists of mother, father, two children, a cook, a nurse, a footman, two postillions, a coachman, two grooms and . . . one more. When the new owner of the dolls' house prods his finger between the closed curtains of the four-poster bed, he feels a *soft shape*; to his alarm he finds 'a white-haired old gentleman in a long linen nightdress and cap' lying quite still. As the story unfolds the house comes to life and mysterious lights appear at the tiny windows, doors open and shut, the bell tolls, and faint cries are heard. If you like frightening books, get *The Collected Ghost Stories of M. R. James* from your local library, and enjoy the full horror of the haunted dolls' house.

But to come back to real life, the dolls' houses in ordinary nurseries in the 1920s and 1930s were mostly rather dull compared with the old Victorian ones. They were not very strongly made, and easily got broken: their metal window frames soon got loose and fell off, and one way and another they quickly became shabby-looking. In spite of this, though, a dolls' house was still a very popular toy, and many thousands were sold each year. Most of the furniture was still made of wood, and some of it was very well finished-off; I have a lovely little bedroom set in my collection, with a bow-fronted chest of drawers, a dressing-table mirror with a drawer for jewellery underneath, a wardrobe complete with doll-size coat-hangers, and a wing armchair, all English-made in the 1930s.

Cardboard furniture was made too – in fact paper and cardboard have always been popular with toymakers, and paper toys can be surprisingly sturdy. Besides the paper theatre in Ann Sharp's house there is also a paper baby-house with paper furniture inside. Paper dolls with wardrobes of different clothes were invented well before 1800, and little boys played with armies of stiff paper soldiers long before metal toy soldiers were mass-produced. We have seen how mid-Victorian

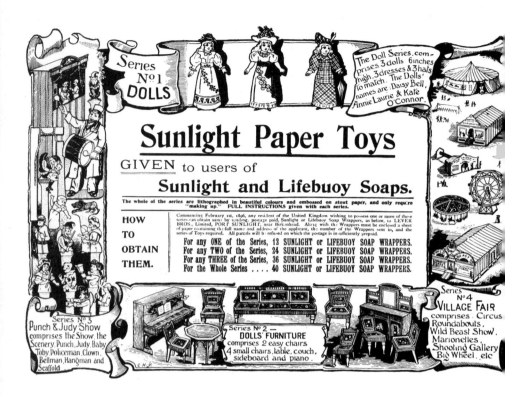

Sunlight Paper Toys

GIVEN to users of

Sunlight and Lifebuoy Soaps.

The whole of the series are lithographed in beautiful colours and embossed on stout paper, and only require "making up." FULL INSTRUCTIONS given with each series.

HOW TO OBTAIN THEM.	Commencing February 1st, 1896, any resident of the United Kingdom wishing to possess one or more of these series can obtain same by sending, postage paid, Sunlight or Lifebuoy Soap Wrappers, as below, to LEVER BROS., Limited, PORT SUNLIGHT, near Birkenhead. Along with the Wrappers must be enclosed a sheet of paper containing the full name and address of the applicant, the number of the Wrappers sent in, and the series of Toys required. All parcels will be refused on which the postage is insufficiently prepaid.
	For any ONE of the Series, 12 SUNLIGHT or LIFEBUOY SOAP WRAPPERS.
	For any TWO of the Series, 24 SUNLIGHT or LIFEBUOY SOAP WRAPPERS.
	For any THREE of the Series, 36 SUNLIGHT or LIFEBUOY SOAP WRAPPERS.
	For the Whole Series .... 40 SUNLIGHT or LIFEBUOY SOAP WRAPPERS.

Series Nº1 DOLLS

The Doll Series comprises 3 dolls 6 inches high, 3 dresses & 3 hats to match. The Dolls' names are Daisy Bell, Annie Laurie & Kate O'Connor.

Series Nº 3 Punch & Judy Show comprises the Show, the Scenery, Punch, Judy, Baby, Toby, Policeman, Clown, Bellman, Hangman and Scaffold

Series Nº 2 — DOLLS' FURNITURE comprises 2 easy chairs 4 small chairs, table, couch, sideboard and piano.

Series Nº 4 VILLAGE FAIR comprises . Circus, Roundabouts, Wild Beast Show, Marionettes, Shooting Gallery, Big Wheel, etc

children put together dolls' house furniture from sections printed on stiff paper sheets, and later on, in 1896, a set of paper furniture – two easy chairs, four small chairs, a table, couch, sideboard and piano – was offered in exchange for twelve Sunlight Soap wrappers. I haven't been able to trace any of this 'free gift' furniture still in existence, but from the drawings in an old 'Sunlight Soap' advertisement it looks very pretty and quite sturdy.

A little cardboard chair probably made in the 1930s is easy to copy, as it only needs two side pieces, a seat and a back, all cut out separately and then glued together. You could trace the shapes I

Part of the model village given away
with 'Instant Whip' pudding.

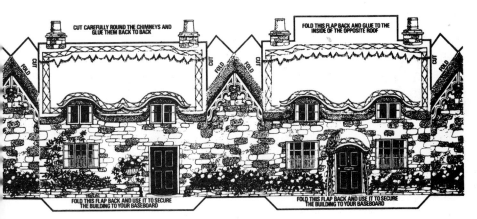

A thatched cottage: the roof would keep this house
warm in winter and cool in summer.

It's not only the dolls' houses of long ago that have interesting stories to go with them. During the Second World War a little girl living in London decided to get her house and its inhabitants ready for the air raids which were then taking place almost every night. She watched her parents preparing their full-size house by putting buckets of sand on the landings in case of fire, and sticking strips of paper onto the window panes to stop splinters of glass flying about if they were broken by bomb-blast. The little girl copied these precautions exactly for her dolls' house, and even built a tiny air raid shelter out of corrugated paper, painted silver, which looked just like metal. Coal was in short supply, so she gave the dolls a little paraffin stove to keep them warm, and plenty of birthday cake candles in case the electricity failed. Heavy 'black-out' curtains were hung at the windows, and the dolls were dressed in cosy one-piece garments called 'Siren Suits', designed especially for wearing in air raid shelters. One doll has an arm-band showing he is an Air Raid Warden, and the lady of the house has her gas-mask, in its cardboard case just like a real one, slung across her shoulder. As a final patriotic touch, the dolls' house is called 'Churchill House' after the great Prime Minister. The interesting thing about this toy is that it gives such a clear picture of just what life was like in wartime London, and it must be the only house – full or doll-size – to have stayed exactly the same since 1940.

From houses like these we can trace all the changes that have taken place in everyday life over the last three hundred years. Candles, either singly in candlesticks or massed in chandeliers, gave way to oil lamps, and these were followed by gas and then electricity. Dolls' house cooking arrangements begin with open fires, spits and roasting jacks; heavy iron ranges come next, often with a tank at the side for hot water; in later kitchens there are miniature gas and electric cookers. Iron cooking pots, brass fenders, copper kettles, wooden butter churns and great domed dish covers (for keeping food warm) are all to be found in old dolls' houses, though in real life most full-size ones were thrown out long ago, and modern dolls' houses, just like real houses, have things like electric mixers and pop-up toasters instead. The dolls' houses of two hundred years ago have elegant Georgian furniture made of walnut or mahogany; later ones are full of Victorian clutter, and for a few short years about 1900 there was even dolls' house furniture made in the fashionable style called *art nouveau*; now we can buy up-to-date things like television sets and tropical fish tanks for our dolls' house sitting rooms. The same sort of changes can be traced in dolls' house bedrooms, where it is still quite usual to see canopied four-poster beds. Bathrooms, of course, are only found in fairly modern doll establishments, since such luxuries were quite unknown in the eighteenth century and for most of the nineteenth. Instead you will see little tin baths in front of the fire in many

dolls' house bedrooms, and marble-topped wash-stands with tiny jugs and basins on them.

The discovery of plastic has made a lot of difference to dolls' house furniture, and in the section on furnishing your house I have made a list of some of the surprising things which toy-makers are now producing. They are every bit as collect-able, in their way, as the sewing tables, the parrot cages and the glass-domed clocks which look so charming in old dolls' houses. It would be interest-ing to equip a modern house with all the gadgets of the 1970s; by the time we get to the 1980s we shall probably think how quaint and old-fashioned they look!

Where to see Dolls' Houses

Of course this is not a complete list of all the dolls' houses on display in the British Isles. I have, though, tried to find houses all over the country, so that wherever you live you should be able to go and see one without too long a journey. It is important to remember that some museums in out-of-the-way places are closed altogether in the winter, and others may only be open on certain days of the week. Often museums are short of space, and a particular dolls' house might not be on view for a few months, while the exhibits are changed round. So before you set out it is a good idea to check that the museum or stately home is in fact open, and the dolls' house on view.

BEDFORDSHIRE
Museum and Art Gallery, Wardown Park, Luton.

BERKSHIRE
Queen Mary's Dolls' House at Windsor Castle.

CAMBRIDGESHIRE
Cambridge and County Folk Museum, 2&3 Castle Street, Cambridge.

CHESHIRE
Grosvenor Museum, Grosvenor Street, Chester.
Stockport Municipal Museum, Turncroft Lane, Vernon Park, Stockport.

DEVON
The Elizabethan House, 70 Fore Street, Totnes (look out for the set of feather furniture).

CO. DURHAM

North of England Open Air Museum, Beamish Hall, Stanley.
The Bowes Museum, Barnard Castle.

ESSEX

Colchester and Essex Museum, The Holly Trees, Colchester.

GLOUCESTERSHIRE

Blaise Castle House Museum, Henbury, Bristol.
Snowshill Manor, near Broadway (National Trust).

HAMPSHIRE

Red House Museum and Art Gallery, Quay Road, Christchurch.

HEREFORDSHIRE

City Museum and Art Gallery, Broad Street, Hereford.

ISLE OF WIGHT

Arreton Manor, near Newport.
Carisbrooke Castle.

KENT

Penshurst Place, near Tonbridge.
Royal Tunbridge Wells Museum and Art Gallery, Civic Centre, Tunbridge Wells. This Museum has a very fine 1840 dolls' house with lovely furniture, and another of about 1890 which originally belonged to a little English girl in Honolulu.
Rochester Museum, Eastgate House, Rochester. One of the dolls' houses here has a brass plate fixed to the front, saying that it was 'Given to Constance H. S. Dahl by Uncle John, August 1882'.

LANCASHIRE

Barry Elder Doll Museum, Carr House, Bretherton.
Queens' Park Art Gallery, Harpurhey, Manchester.
Harris Museum and Art Gallery, Market Square, Preston.
Hill Top, near Sawrey (The National Trust). This was Beatrix Potter's home, and a dolls' house which belonged to her is still there. It isn't the one in *The Tale of Two Bad Mice*, but the plates of food are the same ones which caused the mice so much annoyance.

LONDON
Bethnal Green Museum, Cambridge Heath Road, London, E.2.
Gunnersbury Park Museum, Gunnersbury, London, W.3.
The London Museum, Kensington Palace, London, W.8.
Pollocks Toy Museum, 1 Scala Street, London, W.1. There is a marvellous toy shop here too, selling all kinds of modern dolls' house furniture.

NORFOLK
Strangers' Hall Museum, Charing Cross, Norwich.

NORTHUMBERLAND
Wallington Hall, Cambo, Morpeth (The National Trust).

SOMERSET
The American Museum in Britain, at Claverton Manor, Bath, has a set of miniature rooms.

STAFFORDSHIRE
Museum of Childhood and Costume, Blithfield Hall, Rugeley. The dolls' house is a very important part of this Museum, for it was this house which gave Lady Bagot the idea of forming a toy collection in the first place. It was given to Lady Bagot when she visited Australia in 1960, and is an architect's model of a house built in Adelaide, South Australia, in 1896. The wide verandah and balcony, with its elegant cast-iron work, would give protection in the hot summers. The Museum has lots of other toys, and some very pretty dolls' house furniture.

SURREY
Educational Museum, High Street, Haslemere.

SUSSEX
The Toy Museum, Brighton.
Uppark, South Harting, near Petersfield. Try to visit Uppark on one of the special days when the rooms of the famous babyhouse are opened up. Check this with the National Trust.
Museum and Art Gallery, Chapel Road, Worthing.

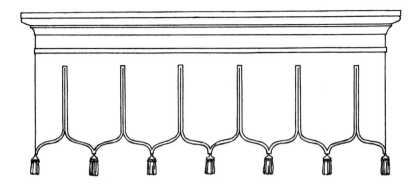

Making Your
Own
Dolls' House

Making Your
Own Dolls' House

Most of the lovely old dolls' houses we have
been looking at are really no more than
glorified cupboards. They are very special cupboards, of course, and all sorts of elaborate woodwork has gone into the making of their miniature
doors and windows, balconies and staircases. But
stripped down to their bare essentials they are still
just cupboards divided into various compartments,
and enclosed by a door or doors. Provided you
aren't too ambitious, and don't set out with the
idea of building something like the Uppark Baby
House, it is quite easy to make a strong, interesting-
looking dolls' house out of an ordinary cardboard
box. No special tools are needed, and all the
necessary materials can usually be found lying
about at home.

The sort of box to look for is the kind used for
packing groceries or other goods; if you ask a local
shopkeeper he is sure to have plenty waiting to be

thrown away, and with luck he will let you take your pick. I got the idea for the first house I made from a box which had held packets of New Zealand butter: it was about 18 inches long, 7 inches deep and 9 inches wide. This is a good size for a two-roomed dolls' house, and I strongly recommend starting off with a similar box. It needn't be exactly the same size, but it *is* important that it should be made from the kind of firm, light cardboard which looks like this:

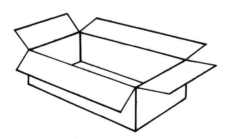

[6] Sectional view of cardboard

As you can see, it has a corrugated layer sandwiched between two smooth layers. Once you have made your first fairly easy house from a box like this, you can go on and tackle more complicated shapes and extra rooms.

To begin with the box looks like this, with the four flaps forming the lid.

[7] A cardboard box, showing flaps

If you stand it on end, though, you can see that it is the foundation of a tall, narrow house; the long flaps will become the doors, one of the short flaps bends back to make the front slope of the roof, and the other short flap is cut off and joined on to make the back part.

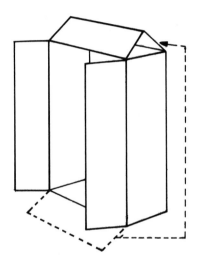

[8] *Cardboard box standing on end, showing how the flaps make doors and roof*

Before going any further, it helps if you can collect together the following materials and tools:

A penknife, or better still a special cutting tool with renewable blades. It looks like this and can be bought very cheaply.

[9] *A cutting tool*

Scissors (but not the best dress-making shears, as the cardboard will blunt them)
A ruler and a sharp pencil
A packet of Polycell or similar wallpaper paste
A roll of strong brown paper strip
A tube of Bostick or other strong glue

Odd pieces of cardboard the same weight and thickness as the main box. It helps if you can pick up two identical boxes, in fact, as this saves a lot of measuring later on.

Various pieces of white and coloured paper – odd lengths of wallpaper, gift-wrapping paper or shelf paper; the covers of old telephone directories are often just the right colour for a roof or a front door. Some thin white card – plain white post-cards are ideal – for door and windows.

A yard of strong white tape about an inch-and-a-half wide, or a strip of any strong white material, for the door hinges.

A paintbrush and a bottle of Indian ink, or a black ballpoint pen or felt pen, for drawing windows and doors.

Two empty match boxes and two corks, for the chimney.

Oddments of felt, woollen material or 'Fablon' for floor coverings.

If possible, but not absolutely necessary: a brass-headed paper fastener, a short length of narrow cotton lace, and a plastic or paper doily. A sheet of paper printed with miniature red bricks, which can be bought for a few pence at most toy or model shops. Sandersons wallpaper shop in London (52 Berners Street, London, W.1.) sells sheets of brick, stone, tile and parquet floor paper specially for dolls' houses.

Although you *can* leave the two long flaps joined on to the box just as they are, I found they opened and shut far better if they were very carefully cut off along the fold with a sharp penknife or cutting tool, and then re-attached to the box with 'hinges' made from the white tape. But if you think this sounds too difficult, or if you are in a great hurry to get your house finished, you can miss out that part from the following step-by-step instructions.

1 Cut off the two long flaps and one of the short flaps, keeping the edges as straight as possible.
2 Bend back the remaining short flap to form half the roof. Attach the other short flap with short lengths of brown sticky paper to make the other half *[10]*.

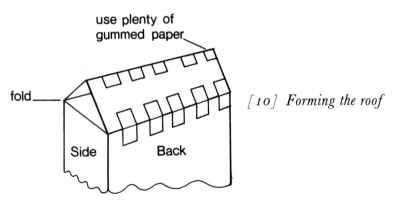

[10] Forming the roof

3 From odd pieces of cardboard, or from the second box, cut two triangles to fit into the

the spaces under the roof. In a real house this part is called the gable. Attach the gables with plenty more sticky tape. This needs a little patience and some help from a grown-up could be useful.

4 Divide the house into two rooms, one up and one down, by putting your ruler inside the box and marking the half-way point on all three walls. Cut thin strips of cardboard from the second box – or any odd pieces – and stick these, with the strong glue, round the inside of the walls at the half-way level. This will form a little ledge on which to rest the floor of the up-stairs room, so it is important to measure most carefully or the floor will slope [11].

5 Cut a rectangle of cardboard the right size for

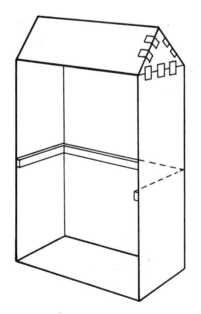

[11] *Dividing the box into two storeys*

The Blackett Baby House (1740) in the London Museum.

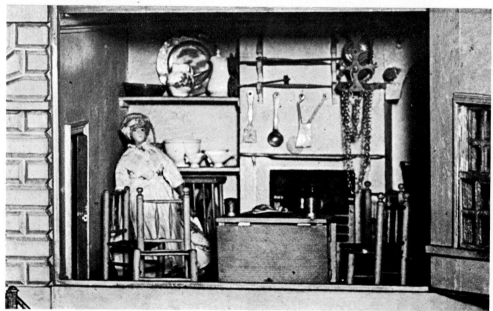

One of the bedrooms and the kitchen in the Blackett Baby House.

the floor, and rest it on the ledge to make sure it fits. Do not stick to the ledge just yet, though, as it is easier to work on the inside of the house without the floor in place.

6 Now for the interesting part: using Polycell, stick wallpaper on the three walls of the upstairs room. It goes on best if you cut three separate oblongs, carefully measured first, rather than trying to stick it on as a single piece. Carry this paper right round the front and about an inch onto the outside walls, so that the raw edge of the cardboard is quite hidden. Paper the downstairs room in exactly the same way. The house begins to look very real if you can find a dark paper for the downstairs, and a lighter, more bedroom-y one, for upstairs [12].

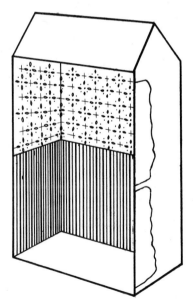

[12] Hanging the wallpaper

Stick white paper (writing paper will do well) on both ceilings, and then fix the bedroom floor (which is also the downstairs ceiling, of course) to the ledge with small blobs of glue.

7 The outside comes next. First, take the two long flaps which have been cut off, and cover them both on one side with either brick paper or any plain white or coloured paper. Carry this round to the back of the doors for at least an inch, neatening the corners rather as if you were doing up a parcel. Use plenty of Polycell, and let it dry completely, preferably under a fairly heavy weight, before the next step.

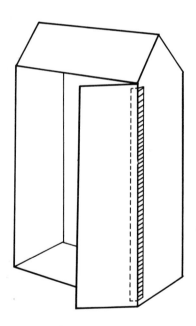

[13] The hinges for the doors

8 The hinges for the doors need care, and again a
  grown-up's help is very useful when you are
  making your first house. Cut two pieces of tape
  to match the height of the doors, fold the tapes
  lengthways down the middle and apply glue
  generously to one half. Stick this to the *back* of
  the door, leaving the other half free to be stuck
  to the *outside* wall of the house after the first lot
  of glue has completely dried *[13]* – not quite as
  complicated as it sounds, as you can see.

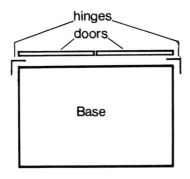

[14] View from underneath

9 Treat the second hinge and the second door in
  the same way. Illustration *[14]* shows what the
  house now looks like from the underneath, so
  you can check that you have got the hinges
  quite right. This is important, otherwise they
  will look clumsy.
10 Using Polycell, cover the side walls with paper
  to match the front, carrying it right up to the

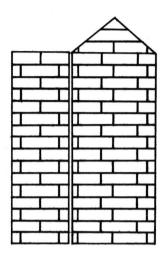

[15] *The side of the house and one of the doors covered with brick paper*

roof, and over the tape hinges at the side *[15]*.

11 Decorate the inside of the doors, using the prettiest paper you can find (coloured wrapping papers are ideal) so that you have an attractive 'frame' for the rooms when the house is open. Cover the tape hinge, which should now be almost completely hidden.

12 The outside of the house needs finishing with some sort of covering for the roof, a front door, windows and a chimney. These can be in any style you like, but the most suitable style for a house of this high, narrow shape is really a terraced town house of the late eighteenth or early nineteenth century. Town houses were usually built to take up as little room along the street front as possible, as the more street

'frontage' a town house had, the more it cost in taxes. So, instead of being wide, town houses were very deep, and a building like our dolls' house would have had other rooms behind, stretching back away from the street, and probably rising up for several storeys and down into a dark basement.

A 'town' dolls' house should have the roof covered with dark grey or blue paper, with lines drawn on it to represent slates. For the doors and windows, copy illustration *[16]*, drawing them on

[16] A 'town' dolls' house

thin white card and then cutting them out. Once you have done one window, you can draw round the shape as many times as necessary – as if you were using a stencil – to make the others. In my house the windows are $4\frac{1}{2}''$ high and the door $8''$ high; I painted the window panes black with Indian ink, leaving the bars white (patience needed again) and stuck narrow lace on at the top to look like pulled-up blinds. The fanlight above the front door is not essential – plenty of houses did not have them – but it does make the house look pretty if you add this extra embellishment. Mine was cut from the middle of a plastic doiley with black paper behind it, and this and a pale blue door (an oblong of stiff paper) were fitted behind a door frame cut from thin white card.

Door and windows should then be stuck on to the front of the house in the appropriate places. The panelling on the front door is just lines drawn on with Indian ink or ballpoint pen, and the real-looking brass door-knob is a paper fastener pushed right through the cardboard. For extra decoration you can add a narrow strip of white card at first-floor level, and perhaps a scalloped strip at roof level. This sort of decoration serves a useful purpose, too, as the easiest way to keep the front shut is to run a length of thin white elastic round the house, and fasten it at the back, out of sight, with a loop and a button. If the elastic rests just above or below the first-floor strip it will be quite unnoticeable, and won't spoil the look of the house at all.

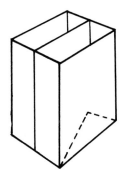

[17] Two matchbox covers make the chimney stack

Two matchbox covers stuck side-by-side are the foundation for the chimney. Cut out triangles *[17]* so that the chimney fits snugly onto the roof, and cover it with brick paper. Brush plenty of Polycell inside the chimney, and then fill it with crumpled tissue paper and more Polycell so that the tissue makes a base for finally fixing it to the roof: a dab of glue will then hold the whole thing firmly in place. The chimney-pots are corks wedged into the upper part of the match-box covers: they too should be fixed with dabs of glue, and painted a reddish-brown colour.

More Complicated Shapes

Once you have seen how to make the first house, you can experiment with boxes of various shapes and sizes and produce all sorts of other styles. Even if you keep to the same shape, you'll see that the 'town house' looks quite different if instead of brick paper you use plain pink paper for the walls, giving it pointed doors and windows like those opposite page 81. This is the 'Gothick' style which became popular from the mid-eighteenth century onwards, as a change from the classical look architects had been copying from Greek and Roman buildings. The designers of 'Gothick' houses based their ideas on the Gothic architecture of the Middle Ages, which is why this little house probably reminds you of a church. You often see old village schools, schoolmasters' houses, chapels and almshouses built in this style, too.

To make a four-roomed house with a wide front you will need a larger box, or you can put two tall narrow boxes together. A helpful wine merchant might be able to find you something suitable, as the sort of boxes used for packing bottles are especially strong, and ideal for dolls-house making. With these bigger boxes the flaps aren't always the right size or in the right place for making the roof and fronts, but don't worry about this so long as the main part of the box will provide the back, sides, top and bottom; the roof and fronts can easily be cut from a separate box.

One word of warning before you start: don't choose a box which will make your house too deep from front to back, or the rooms too low. It is difficult to arrange dolls' house furniture unless you can reach the back of the room without knocking over the things in front, and if the ceilings are too low you won't be able to see inside very well, and the whole effect will be spoiled. When you look at an old dolls' house, notice how the rooms are nearly always a little taller in proportion to their width and depth than they would be in real life.

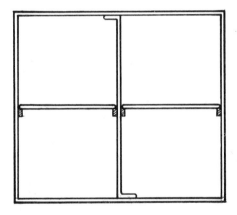

[18] A box divided into four rooms
For the upright middle division, take a piece of
cardboard the same height as the house, and as
wide as the house is deep. A narrow flap at the
top and bottom will hold it in position.

Once a suitable box has been found it should be divided into four rooms as shown here *[18]*. The divisions are made of cardboard, the upright piece

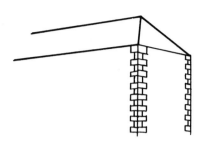

[*19*] *A hipped roof*

being glued into position first. Then ledges are stuck on to support the upstairs floor, just as they were for the narrow town house.

Make the roof next. If you look at real houses you will see that roofs are generally either just two sloping sides, with two straight gables, like the town house roof, or *four* sloping sides, like this one [*19*]. This sort is called a 'hipped' roof, and it is quite easy to copy for a dolls' house, especially if you know a little about geometry and can work out the right measurements. There are no gables to a 'hipped' roof, as the small triangles at the side come right down to the top of the main wall.

When the roof is on firmly, the next step is to decorate the rooms with ceiling and wall papers, overlapping any rough cardboard edges as you go along. This means carrying the wallpapers round to the outside walls, and the ceiling papers up onto the floor above for an inch or so. By the time one of these cardboard dolls' houses is finished there shouldn't be anything at all of the original box to be seen, and all the cut edges should be neatly covered with paper.

Now for the front: if you can find a piece of cardboard to fit right across the front so much the better. This means that only one hinge is needed, and you can make a simple fastening on the opposite side out of a paper fastener and some fine string, as shown here [20]. Otherwise your house can have a front opening in two halves, like the tall town house.

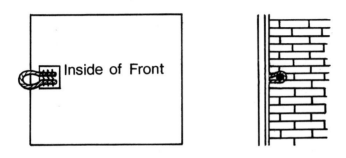

[20] The fastening
The string loop should be sewn onto a small piece of fabric, and then the whole thing glued to the inside edge of the door.

All these houses, whatever their size and shape, are better if they are glued to a base board when they are finished. The base board should be cut from a piece of cardboard about an inch bigger all round than the floor area of the house, and covered with plain paper. If the house is then glued to the middle of this base it will not only look nicer but it will also stand up better, without tipping over.

With these two basic shapes – tall and narrow or lower and wide – you can design almost any type of house. Britain has so many different styles of building that it would be interesting to make a dolls' house to match the traditional building style of your own part of the country. Although modern houses are all apt to look alike, with brick walls and slate roofs, there are still plenty of old houses left with their own very definite regional styles. Before the days of canals and railways it was difficult to transport heavy loads, and people had to rely on whatever building materials happened to be close by – stone from a local quarry if they were lucky, otherwise bricks if they had the right sort of clay for making them, or timber or flint or even mud. Pictures and photographs of different sorts of houses can be found in guidebooks and books on architecture in any Public Library. If you collect stamps, have a careful look at the charming series which the Post Office issued in 1970 showing traditional country buildings from Scotland, the English Cotswolds, Ireland and Wales: they would all make interesting dolls' houses. The ordinary Telephone Directories have drawings of local buildings on the first dozen or so pages – not many people seem to have noticed them, but they are all excellent and the artists have included lots of pretty little houses which you could copy. Estate Agents' announcements, advertisements and magazine articles are other places to look for ideas, and of course you can always go out and look at the real houses in the district where you live. Even in a busy, modern-looking High Street it's surprising how many old buildings there are still to be seen if you look above the new shop-fronts. If you go abroad on holiday, make a drawing of a typical house – a fisherman's cottage, perhaps, with a red pantiled roof and brightly painted walls, and turn it into an unusual dolls' house when you get back home. Or be really adventurous and copy a Canadian log cabin (remember how Victorian children made miniature Swiss chalets covered with split twigs), or one of those delightful Australian houses with verandahs and cast iron balconies. Once you begin to think about it, there are literally hundreds of different ways of building a house, and just as many ways of making a dolls' house. In the next few pages I have drawn some designs to give you one or two ideas, but you will be able to find and copy many other styles for yourselves.

A granite cottage in the north of England

A typical weather-boarded house in Kent

A gamekeepers thatched cottage

A Norfolk Cottage

Cob is a mixture of mud, water and straw, and it is one of the oldest English building materials. It may not sound very strong, but in fact small houses with walls made of cob have lasted for hundreds of years, especially in Devonshire and other parts of the South-west. There is a saying that all cob needs is 'a good hat and a good pair of shoes' – meaning an overhanging thatched roof to protect it from the rain, and a layer of stone at the foot of the walls to. stop the damp spreading upwards from the ground. If you are ever anywhere near Milton Abbas, in Dorset; go and look at the village street bordered by neat cob houses which were built as late as 1790: they were put up by the local squire who wanted to provide the villagers with new homes well away from his own park, where he felt their humble little houses spoiled the view!

To make a cob dolls' house, start off with the basic long four-roomed shape. Real cob houses are usually plastered over and white-washed, to give the mud walls extra protection from the weather, so the dolls' house should have white walls. A special sort of 'woodchip' wallpaper has a rough, knobbly surface which is ideal for cob walls: you may be able to find a piece left over from some home-decorating, or a wallpaper shop might have an old pattern book to spare. The doors and windows should be very simple shapes, and not too big. The roof must look as if it is thatched, with a long steep

[21] *A cob house*

slope and a good overhang.

This is the main snag, as if you make a dolls' house with an overhanging roof you can't get the front open – the bottom of the roof gets in the way. The easiest way of solving the problem is to have a *fixed* front, and to open the house at the *back*. This is a trick which many dolls' house builders evidently found useful in the past, as I have seen quite a few houses with openings at the back or sides instead of at the front.

Thatch is another challenge. It ought really to be made of straw, and if you are in the country at the right time of year you can probably beg a few handfuls from a farmer after he has finished harvesting. Otherwise raffia makes a good substitute, or dried grasses can be used.

[22] *How to make a projection for the roof*

As with the other houses, the foundation for the roof is cardboard, and a 'hipped' roof would be especially suitable. To make the overhang at the front and sides, glue on a fairly wide extra strip to project well out beyond the main roof [22]. Add the chimney next, either in the middle of the roof ridge or at one end of the house. When you are satisfied with the general shape, cover the whole roof with 'thatch', using the following method:

From a short length of any old cotton material, cut out pieces which exactly match the shape and size of the cardboard roof sections. Lay the pieces of material down flat, and then arrange the straw, raffia or grass in a fairly thick layer on each section. Thread a big needle with a long strand of raffia or thin string and then, keeping the 'thatch' as flat as possible, make two lines of giant cross-stitching to hold it in place on the cotton material. Finally, glue the separate sections, material side down, to the cardboard roof, and there you are.

A Timber-Framed House

Originally nearly all the small houses for ordinary people in Britain were made of a wooden frame filled in with anything that was handy – small twigs woven together, mud, or bricks. There used to be many more forests than there are now, so there was no shortage of oak, one of the best woods for building as it gets harder and harder with age. There are plenty of timber-framed houses still lived in which have been standing for four hundred years, and this style of architecture is so well-loved in England that quite modern houses in suburbs and along by-passes often have thin strips of wood nailed to the outside in imitation of much older buildings.

The basic timber framework of the old houses was much the same all over the country, but people living in different regions finished them off in various special ways. All over the West Midlands, and especially in Cheshire, the wooden beams make striking 'black-and-white' patterns, and the carpenters went to a lot of trouble to shape the timbers so that they would form elaborate designs against the white plaster filling. The most famous example of this style is Little Moreton Hall, in Cheshire, which was built in the sixteenth century.

You will find a picture of this lovely building in almost any book on English architecture, and although the whole house would be rather too complicated to turn into a dolls' house it would be easy to copy some of the patterns made by the dark beams.

Decide on the pattern first, and unless it is going to be a very simple one it is best to try it out on a sheet of paper before sticking the various strips and curves onto the walls of your dolls' house. The walls themselves should first be covered with white paper, and the timbers cut out of black paper. Windows should be small, and might have diamond-shaped panes, and the roof should be made of thatch like the cob house, or covered with reddish-orange tiles cut out separately, one by one.

In parts of East Anglia, especially Essex and Suffolk, timber-framed houses were treated in a quite different way. Here the wooden framework and the filling were usually covered over completely with a thick layer of plaster, which helped to keep out draughts and cold, so that the walls were white all over, with no dark beams showing. The plaster covering was made from very strange-sounding ingredients – lime, sand, cow hair and dung, bits of straw and water – all mixed together. The mixture was spread on the walls, and before it dried lovely sweeping patterns of leaves, flowers, stars or just squiggles were drawn on with a pointed stick or pressed out with a wooden mould like a giant butter pat. These decorations are known as

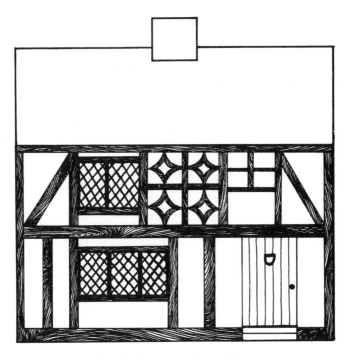

[23] *A timber-framed house*

'pargetting', and many houses treated in this way in the seventeenth century are still as good as new; if you ever visit Clare, in Suffolk, you can see some very beautiful and famous pargetting, but there is plenty more to be discovered in other parts of Suffolk and around Saffron Walden in Essex.

I thought these houses were so pretty I decided to make a dolls' house like them. At first I was rather puzzled about how I could imitate pargetting without a supply of cow-hair and all the rest of the old materials, but after a few experiments I found that a white plastic lace mat was a perfect substitute; a paper doiley or some embossed

85

wallpaper, or even a piece of ordinary white lace would do just as well, stuck to the wall and then covered with a coat of white emulsion paint.

This dolls' house was quite a complicated one and took me several days to make; this was partly because I gave it proper cut-out windows instead of simply sticking window shapes on to the walls. The window 'glass' came from the stiff transparent lid of a box which had originally held some 'Notelets', but various other things like soap and bath salts are often packed in similar boxes. Real-looking windows like this are rather nice additions, and if you decide to tackle a house of this kind it will help if you do things in the following order:

1 Make the basic four-roomed, long, low foundation, and build up the roof shape. Paper the rooms.

2 Cut out the front or fronts in plain cardboard, and decide where you want the windows, which should not be too big in a house of this age and type. Cut holes in the front where the windows are to be.

3 Cover the front with white paper, neatening the edges of the window holes.

4 Cover the area to be pargetted (remembering to leave a space for the front door) with parts of a white plastic lace mat. Use Polycell for sticking, as some glues dissolve the plastic.

5 Cut window frames out of stiff black paper, making them a little bigger all round than the

[24] A diamond-paned window

window holes. Stick the transparent 'glass'
behind the frames, and mark small panes on
each window. This can be done either by drawing a diamond pattern on with a fine paintbrush
and grey model paint, or by sticking on fairly
thick thread in the same criss-cross pattern. It *is*
rather fiddly to do, I must admit, but I can pass
on one hint which makes it easier: a good way of
getting the lines of the panes even is to draw the
pattern on a piece of spare paper, and then put
the 'glass' on top of this and either paint the
panes or stick on the thread to correspond with
the lines underneath. Illustration *[24]* shows the
finished diamond-paned window should look,
but of course the same method can be adapted
for any other size and style.

6 Glue these window frames, with the windows
inside, over the gaps in the front cut ready for
them.

7 Stick on a front door made from thick paper,

and a plain door-frame round it. As this is an old house which has had a lot of use, I cut out a hollow in the front door step to make it look as if it had been worn down by generations of people going in and out.

8 Attach the front, or fronts, to the basic house with tape hinges.

9 Cover the outside of the side walls with white paper, hiding the tape hinges. Add fancy bargeboards to the gables where the roof meets the wall.

10 Cover the inside of the front with any pretty paper.

11 Cover the roof with small tiles cut out separately from reddish-brown and orange paper. If you want the roof to look as if it is made of pantiles, cover it first with corrugated paper, and then stick separate paper tiles over this, pressing them well down into the ridges.

12 Give the house a low matchbox chimney, covered with brick paper, and stick in two small corks or round pencil stubs to represent chimney-pots.

In Sussex and Kent, and some other parts of the South-East, timber-framed houses are different again. Here the builders have cased the whole building with horizontal wooden planks, called clapboarding, to protect the walls from the weather. A dolls' house of this type should have long strips of white card pasted right across the front, each strip slightly overlapping the one underneath it. By the time this style became popular sash windows were quite common, so the dolls' house can have these bigger windows regularly spaced out. The roof should be made of reddish tiles, and the chimney should be of brick.

Surrey has timber-framed houses with small, light tiles hanging on the walls as a protection. These tiles were often made in fancy shapes, and hung in regular patterns, so that they look like fish-scales. This is an easy look to copy for a dolls' house, as the tiles can be cut out from stiffish paper and then stuck on row by row, overlapping each other.

A Cotswold House

Most Cotswold houses are built of the local limestone, which is a lovely yellow-greyish colour. This
stone is excellent for building, being neither too
hard nor too soft, and a belt of it runs right across
England in a diagonal line from Lincolnshire to
Dorset.

In the Middle Ages stone was only used for
important buildings like churches and large
mansions, but by about 1600 – provided there was a
quarry within reach – quite small houses were
being built of stone. At this time the Cotswolds were
famous for sheep, and the wool trade meant that
the local farmers and merchants were very rich, and
built themselves beautiful houses. Witney in
Oxfordshire is still famous for blanket-making, and
if you look at the labels on the blankets on your bed
there's a good chance you will find they were made
in one of the mills there.

A Cotswold farmhouse converts very well into a
dolls' house, and the first thing to do is to find the
right colour for the walls. Some model shops sell
sheets of 'stone' paper which are quite suitable, or
art shops and stationers' usually stock sheets of
plain coloured paper known as 'sugar' paper. The
roof of a real Cotswold house is made of tiles cut
from the same limestone as the walls, giving the
roofs an attractive wavy look quite different from
the smooth blue slates of town houses; for the dolls'
house each tile should be cut out separately, some

90

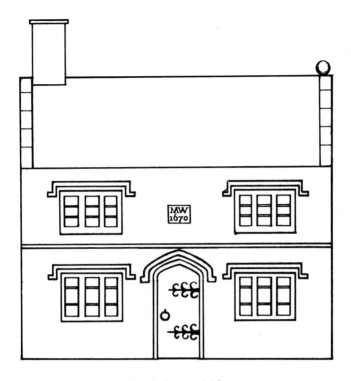

[25] *A Cotswold house*

from the same paper as the walls and others from the grey cardboard at the back of a writing pad, which will give slight variations in colour and thickness. After the tiles are stuck on you can add some small patches of dark brown paint to represent tight, velvety moss growing here and there. People living in houses like this used to encourage moss to grow on the roof to help keep out draughts and snow. To make sure the rain runs off quickly the roof slope is always steep, otherwise water would find its way through the gaps between the small stone tiles.

Cotswold builders paid great attention to the gables, so a Cotswold dolls' house ought to look as nice as possible from the side, with perhaps a small window high up near the roof. Another way of making the gable important was to finish it off at the top with a stone decoration like a ball: I used a large round wooden bead for the dolls' house version.

Chimneys should be tall and square, without chimney pots. One matchbox cover is not high enough, so I used two, kept together by sliding a matchbox tray half-way through each cover, and then stuck two pairs together side-by-side to get the right square-ish look.

Now for the doors and windows. Cotswold windows are set between heavy stone divisions called mullions, and the panes of glass are quite small, as you can see from the drawing. The flat stone 'hat' over the window, and the raised strip running all round the house, are called 'dripstones', and these and the window frames should all be cut out separately from sugar paper and stuck on. Even chimneys often had a raised strip running round them near the top, and this can be copied, too.

The front door should be darkish brown, to look like oak, with black iron hinges drawn on. The ring handle can be drawn on, or a small picture-hanging ring, if you can find one, looks very realistic. The door surround is stone, like the window frames, and should be cut out in sugar paper, and so should the dripstone 'hat' over the door.

These houses often have a square stone above the door, with the date and the initials of the first proud owner carved on it. I put 1670 on my Cotswold dolls' house, as this seemed about right for its regular front and evenly-spaced windows.

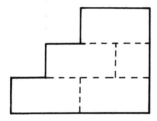

[26] *A mounting-block*

You will probably have all sorts of ideas for other finishing touches. I thought of adding a mounting block, which is a short flight of stone steps to help people, especially the elderly, get on to their horses. You can make one from five matchboxes (one of them cut in half), stuck together [26] and then covered with stone-coloured paper to match the rest of the house, and finally glued on at the side. Another 'extra' is a bread oven, which used to be an important part of a farmhouse kitchen, and which stretched so far back into the wall that it stuck out on the outside in a small rounded bulge, with its own little tiled roof. You still often see them in villages, especially if you go round to the back of the old houses. It is quite an easy shape to build up in

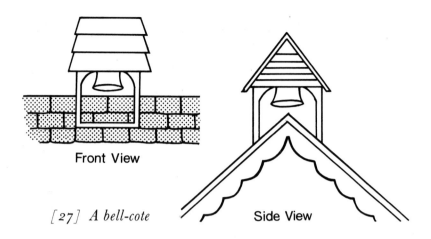

Front View

[27] *A bell-cote*   Side View

cardboard, or you might come across a cardboard tube or canister – something like 'Vim' canister would do well, cut in half down the middle.

Something else which you still see on old houses in the country is a bell-cote, like schools used to have, with a bell hanging inside which could be rung to call workers in from the fields for their meals. This is more difficult to make than the other 'extras' as it means constructing a tiny framework with a pointed roof on top of it, and then fixing it securely to the very top of the house, near the chimneys. The illustration *[27]* shows the shape to aim for, and it is possible to build it up out of balsa wood or to use parts of a matchbox cover, and then add a roof made from a piece of folded card. The easiest part is the bell itself, as you can buy dear little bells from shops which sell wedding cake decorations, and hang one under the roof on a piece of cotton.

Another *very* easy addition from the wedding

94

cake department is a lucky horseshoe for fixing above the dolls' house front door; to look really genuine it ought to be painted black, like iron, but apart from that all it needs is a dab of glue.

A Georgian House

This has always been the favourite style for dolls' house builders, and no wonder. The regular flat front, with a central front door and windows spaced out evenly on either side of it, is by far the easiest to copy. Whether a dolls' house is a grand affair like the Tate Baby House in the Bethnal Green Museum, or a much humbler home-made one from a Victorian nursery, the style is still what architects call 'Georgian'.

Strictly speaking, a 'Georgian' house is one built during the reigns of the first four King Georges, which lasted from 1714 to 1830. But the style was so popular, and is so especially suitable for rows of town houses joined together in terraces, that it has never really gone out of fashion, and many new houses today are still designed on Georgian lines. Things to look out for in real houses of this type, and to copy for a dolls' house, are tall sash windows with all the woodwork painted white, and an elegant front door, perhaps with pillars at the side and a fanlight above. Walls were smooth stone, or regular brickwork sometimes covered with 'stucco' (a kind of plaster) to make them smoother still. To get an uncluttered, oblong look to the front of a house architects used to hide the roof as best they could by building up the front wall to cut it off from view. This extra piece of wall is called a parapet, and it was something dolls' house builders were quick to copy since it often saved them the trouble of making a roof at all. Many old dolls' houses were just left with a flat top, quite un-decorated and chimney-less, hidden behind an ornamental parapet.

To make this parapet, you must have the front slightly higher than the rest of the house, so if you are using the flaps of a box for the fronts you will have to build them up with a separate strip of cardboard. The join won't matter at all, as most real parapets are decorated with horizontal lines of ornamental brick or stonework, and the join simply becomes one of these lines.

If the middle part of the front wall rises up to form a flattish triangle (a 'pediment' in architect's language), this might have some extra decoration. If you look at the photograph of Sarah Lethieullier's baby-house you will see that the pediment has her family's coat-of-arms and a lot of ornamental carving on it. In Norfolk I have seen a real house with a picture of some sheep carved in this three-cornered space. In other houses you might see a small round window (probably the window of the maids' bedroom, as the poor girls usually had to sleep in pokey attics) or a clock – both easy ideas to copy for a dolls' house. You can even cut a round

hole in the pediment and borrow a man's pocket
watch to hang behind it to give the right time.

An Australian House

Just as the lovely old Cotswold houses were built by
rich English wool merchants so, two and three
hundred years later, elegant houses were built on
the other side of the world by the owners of
Australian sheep stations. Captain John Macarthur
was a great pioneer who probably did more than
anyone else to establish the wool industry in
Australia, for it was he who brought the famous
Merino sheep to Australia from South Africa and
Britain. In 1793, only five years after the first
British settlers had arrived, he built Elizabeth
Farm House, a long low homestead with white walls
and a cool, wide verandah paved with flag-stones.
This interesting house is still standing today, one of
the oldest buildings in Australia; in fact it has
become a celebrated national monument and been
turned into a museum illustrating the history of
sheep farming.

The early Australian builders designed houses
with an English look, like the ones so many of the

settlers had left behind. They had to make several important changes, though: for example, in Victorian times at least one imposing Australian homestead was built with an observation tower on top which was used as a lookout in case of unfriendly aborigines! Many buildings were given corrugated iron roofs to stand up to the heavy rains, and very often there are wide verandahs and balconies – also with corrugated iron roofs – to keep off the hot sun. One of the prettiest things about these buildings is the cast-iron work, just like lace, on porches, verandahs and sometimes rooftops. Tons and tons of this 'iron lace' was put up all over Australia in the nineteenth century; some of it was brought out from England, carried in sailing ships for ballast, but a great deal was made in Australia too, for it was immensely fashionable to have a house decorated in this way.

The easiest way to copy this cast-iron work on a dolls' house is just to substitute lengths of ordinary cotton lace, or pieces cut from a lacey plastic mat. You can buy lace very cheaply in most drapers' shops: it comes in lots of different widths and patterns, and you will need, if possible, about a yard of very narrow edging for the 'frills' at the top of the verandahs, and something wider (say about three inches wide for an average dolls' house) for the balconies.

Even the iron footscrapers placed outside the front doors were cast in the same lacey patterns.

[28] *An Australian House*

[29] *Footscraper at Elizabeth Farm House,*
Parramatta, Australia

This is a drawing [29] of one of the scrapers at
Elizabeth Farm House: trace the design onto thin
card, cut it out carefully, and paint it black. It
doesn't matter about cutting out the little spaces in
the middle – the scraper will look quite all right if
they are left white.

The corrugated iron roof is no problem if you
make it from ordinary corrugated paper. Paint it
with two coats of grey or black gloss paint, which
will give it a hard 'metallic' look, or use varnish
over poster paint or thin coloured paper to get
much the same effect.

When I made the house in the drawing, I did
things in the following order, and if you decide on
an Australian house I think you will find it simplest
if you do the same:

1 Make the basic shape, and paper the inside walls.
2 If you want white 'iron lace', have grey or beige
   outside walls, so that the lace will show up. If you
   have black ironwork then the walls can be white.
3 Stick on the doors and windows.
4 Add balconies and verandahs by sticking on
   strips of lace, as if you were building up a collage.

5 Cover roof slopes with corrugated paper (ridged side up), and either paint it or cover it with thin coloured paper pressed well down into the ridges.

Some Unusual Houses to Make

There's no need to copy an ordinary house when you plan your dolls' house. There have always been people who built real houses quite different from the ones their neighbours lived in, and it's fun to copy some of their ideas. The eighteenth and early nineteenth centuries were the great years for unusual buildings; while most rich people wanted to live in classical, flat-fronted mansions with neat sash windows, there were a few eccentric land-owners who rebelled against this fashion and built themselves extraordinary houses which looked like churches, or Indian temples, or old castles with battlements and turrets. An enormously rich man called William Beckford built himself a huge house at Fonthill in Wiltshire which was a copy of Salisbury Cathedral! Two gangs of workmen laboured night and day for eleven years to get it finished, but no sooner was it completed than the great tower, 225 feet high, collapsed to the ground. Poor Mr. Beckford got thoroughly fed up with Fonthill after that, and decided to go and live in Bath. But even then he wasn't cured of tower-building, for he built another called Lansdowne Tower; this was evidently much stronger, as it is still standing today.

Nothing could be more out of the ordinary than the Prince Regent's Pavilion at Brighton with all its oriental domes, and if you ever spend a holiday on the Sussex coast you should certainly go and see it. Another fantastic house, but in a very different style, was built about the same time at Eagle, in Lincolnshire. It was called 'The Jungle', and had its door and window frames made from rough tree trunks and branches; the whole thing was soon covered with matted ivy, but apparently it was considered very charming indeed as one of its first visitors called it a 'tasty' home. The owner added to its oddness by keeping a menagerie in the garden – deer, pheasants, buffaloes and kangaroos. The locals probably thought him most eccentric, though a lot of people *were* eccentric at that time, and didn't mind at all about being thought 'different' from their neighbours.

Even if a country gentleman lived in an ordinary house himself, the chances were that he built a 'folly' or two in his grounds – a garden temple perhaps (have you ever seen the Chinese Pagoda in Kew Gardens?) or some artificial ruins to provide an interesting view from the drawing room windows. Ladies occupied themselves in decorating rooms with wonderfully intricate patterns of shells in shades of pink, mauve, black and white. This work often took them several years, and cargoes of shells reached England from all over the world. The most delightful little house with the enchanting name of 'A la Ronde', near Exmouth, was the home of two cousins, Jane and Mary Parminter, who decorated the rooms by sticking thousands and thousands of shells and feathers on the walls. They used some of the feathers most cleverly to make portraits of birds, and the whole effect is quite charming. Like the Brighton Pavilion, this unusual house is open to the public now, so don't miss it if you are ever anywhere near.

There are still pretty decorated lodges to be seen all over the country, standing beside drive gates or at the entrance to a park. As they are small, often with only one storey, they are quite easy to convert into dolls' houses.

The really enthusiastic folly-builders, though, were not content with lodges and sham ruins and rooms lined with shells. What they went in for were grottoes, the darker and damper the better, if possible built beside a lake and furnished with a few rough tree stumps. Having constructed their grottoes, they then advertised in the newspapers for genuine hermits to come and live in them. One gentleman wanted his hermit to occupy an underground grotto for seven years, without speaking or shaving. In return the hermit was offered a good supply of books to read, an organ to play on, delicious food from the big house and fifty pounds a year; in spite of these rewards, though, we are told he only stuck to the job for four years. Another hermit called Carolus was more contented, for he lived happily in his grotto at Tong in Shropshire for many years, until his death in 1822. His employer, George Durant, was a celebrated folly-builder, and as well as Carolus's comfortable grotto he dotted his estate with all sorts of pedestals, lodges, archways and monuments to favourite animals. Even the coal-house was lavishly decorated, but his greatest masterpiece was a pyramid-shaped brick hen-house, twenty feet high and with four storeys, called the Egyptian Aviary. It was covered with carving – a swan swimming along amongst some rushes and a cat carrying a kitten in her mouth were particularly appealing – and inscriptions like 'Scratch before you Peck' and 'Better Come Out of the Way Love' for the benefit of the hens.

I don't think a hermit dolls' house would be very attractive, but a miniature shell grotto would be charming and quite quick and easy to do. You could begin with an ordinary shape, but decorate it with shells collected at the seaside. The roof should be all flat shells, arranged like tiles, and the windows and door could be bordered with rows of tiny round ones. More rows of shells could be stuck on just underneath the roof and at first-floor level, and down each side of the front. But try out your design before you begin sticking, as like the eighteenth century ladies who built grottoes you will find shells go a surprisingly short way once you start arranging them in patterns.

A Six-Sided Summer-House

So far we have only been thinking of unusual dolls'
houses made from oblong boxes. If you can spare
the time and trouble, however, you can do what I
did and make a most successful little six-sided
summer-house. It was based on a box which had
held triangular cardboard cartons of milk – you
will know the kind of box I mean when I say it is the
same shape as a patch in a patchwork quilt. Your
milkman or local dairy can almost certainly let you
have one, as they are generally thrown away when
they are empty.

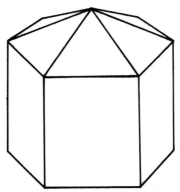

[30]   The basic 'summer-house' shape

When you look at the box you'll see that the
bottom isn't flat, but sticks up in the middle in a
point. The first thing to do is to push the point
outwards to make the roof. You will have to unfasten
part of the box for this, and then stick the six roof
sections back into position with strips of strong
sticky paper. You now have the basic shape,

though at this stage the summer-house has no floor and no openings in the sides *[30]*.

The next step is to find a large sheet of cardboard – the side of any really big carton will do – and stand the summer-house on it. Draw round the six sides with a sharp pencil, and then cut out this giant piece of patchwork; cut slightly *inside* the pencil lines, so that the 'patch' will fit into the summer-house to make the floor. Try it for size, but don't glue it into position yet.

For a flat ceiling you will need another piece of cardboard exactly the same as the floor, or the roof can be left just as it is inside, going up to a point in the middle. If you do decide to have a flat ceiling, this is the time to glue it in.

Next, draw yet another patch exactly like the first one, putting it in the middle of another sheet of cardboard. Don't cut round this outline, but lie a ruler against it and draw another 'patch' round it. Cut round this outer line, and then stick the smaller,

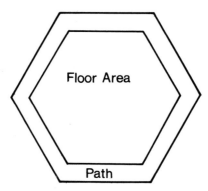

[31] *diagram showing the lay-out of the summer-house floor*

first patch in the middle of this second larger one. This will make the floor of the summer-house, and a little path, the width of your ruler, all round it [31].

As I wanted to make a real dolls' house and not just a model, there had to be a way of opening the summer-house and getting furniture and dolls into it. Doors are not very practical for a six-sided building, so I decided instead to turn the three back walls into open archways. From the front the summer-house looks quite solid, but when you move round to the back you can see straight through the archways into its one room, and put your hand inside to move the furniture about.

After the inside walls have been papered the whole of the upper part – the walls and the roof – can be glued to the base. Put some blobs of strong glue on the base round the edge of the floor piece, and press the upper part down on to it. Make sure the floor fits *inside* the walls all the way round, as this helps to hold everything together firmly.

All this sounds complicated, but if you follow the instructions carefully and look at the diagrams it is not much more difficult to make this house than an ordinary oblong one. The outside can be finished off in all sorts of different ways, and it is a particularly good shape for turning into a dolls' 'folly'.

I based the outside of mine on one of those china ornaments in the shape of a cottage. I'm sure you know the sort of thing I mean – you often see them in antique dealers' windows. They usually have masses of flowers all round, and a chimney in the middle of the roof. Often the doors and windows are pointed, like those of the 'Gothick' house, and sometimes there is a sheep with twin lambs in the garden. I copied all these ideas for my summer-house, and if you want to do the same I think you will find the following suggestions helpful.

Chimney A piece of postcard 1″ high and 4″ long, marked off into six equal ¾″ lengths and then joined together to make a six-sided chimney stack. The chimney pot is a small cork, held in place with a papier mâché mixture made from a face tissue soaked in Polycell (a most useful substance, by the way, for all sorts of 'filling' jobs).

Roof This can be covered with printed tile paper, any coloured paper, thatch, or – prettiest of all – shells.

Walls Stone, brick or plain paper of any colour.

Doors and Windows Almost any shape would do for a 'folly' house like this, but pointed 'Gothick' shapes are perhaps the most appropriate. If you have chosen a shell roof, outline the door and windows with more shells.

Doorstep A small block of wood – balsa wood is ideal – can be stuck onto the garden path outside the front door to make a step.

Garden Cover the path with green paper, over-lapping the edge to neaten it. Build up a garden with small artificial flowers, and paint others climbing up the walls. Make a trellis on part of one wall with a criss-cross of matchsticks, or thin strips of balsa wood, or white card. A real twig, if it is the right shape, can be stuck to one wall to make a tree, with blossom and leaves made from beads, paper or very small artificial flowers and attached with blobs of glue. A few stones or shells can be stuck to the pathway – tiny rounded stones can be arranged to look like cobblestones. Dried moss and grasses are useful for filling in gaps, and if you know anyone who grows old-fashioned 'everlasting' flowers ask if you can have a bunch, as they look even better than artificial flowers.

Keep the main part of the garden in the front, leaving the open arches at the back uncluttered so that you can get furniture in and out without crushing any tall flowers.

Animals   The little plastic sheep and lambs sold for farmyard sets look very pretty in the garden, or you might be able to find one or two of the traditional toy sheep with thin wooden legs and white woolly bodies. Of course you don't have to choose sheep, though for some reason these seem to have been the most popular animals with the makers of the china cottages. Cats or rabbits or hens would be just as suitable, dotted about amongst the flowers.

While we're on the subject of cats . . . well, you can't keep them out of a book about dolls' houses any more than you can keep them out of real dolls' houses. My cat is perfectly at home in my Victorian model: she squeezes in through the front door and into the hall, and then turns sharply into either the dining room or the kitchen and sits looking out from behind the muslin curtains, blinking her round yellow eyes. As soon as I begin making a new dolls' house she takes a great interest, jumping in and out of the various cardboard boxes, and then settling down for a good sleep in some half-finished sitting-room. All cats seem to like having a cosy box-shaped place of their own, especially if it has a roof and keeps off all the draughts, and if you have a cat you might think about adapting one of the dolls' house designs to suit it.

In fact a house for a cat is much easier and quicker to make than a dolls' house, as it only needs three sides, a floor and a roof – in other words, the basic dolls' house shape but without any doors to bother with. The back is left open for the cat to get in and out, and the floor should be covered with a folded piece of soft material to make a bed. The other sides should be decorated like the outside of a house, and the roof finished off like any of the dolls' houses we have been looking at. For a really luxurious look the inside walls can be papered, and a few kitten portraits stuck on.

The outside can be in any style you like, but I have come across a very attractive real house which would convert especially well into a home for either cats or dolls. It is a black-and-white building at Henfield, in Sussex, and it is actually known as 'The Cat House'. It has a thatched roof, and underneath, in the white squares between the black timbers, is a row of black cat silhouettes, running all round the house like a frieze. Long ago

it was occupied by an old lady who was very fond of her canary. Nearby lived the Vicar, who was very fond of his cat; the cat used to go with him to church, and on the way they had to pass the old lady's house. One day – as you've probably guessed already – the canary was outside, and the cat snapped it up and killed it. The old lady was so cross that she had an effigy of the cat made, and hung it outside her house so that every time the Vicar passed he was reminded of his cat's cruelty. Later on, when the old lady had died and the Cat House had a new owner, the cat silhouettes were painted high up on the walls to commemorate the sad story. If you ever go to Henfield you can see the house, near the church; look carefully, and you will notice that every cat is holding an unfortunate canary. This would make an unusual decoration for a half-timbered dolls' house; there is no need to draw each cat separately, as if you have a piece of tracing paper you can just reproduce the first drawing as many times as necessary.

A 'Pre-Fab'

Not all unusual houses are old. There are plenty of
people nowadays who build themselves very strange
homes, or who convert windmills or lighthouses or
railway coaches and go and live in them very
happily. At the end of the Second World War,
when houses were in terribly short supply, someone
had the brilliant idea of putting up temporary
buildings made of prefabricated sections. This
meant that the walls, roof, door and windows were
all made piece by piece in a factory, and these
various sections only needed fixing together in the
towns where they were wanted. Families could
then move in immediately, instead of having to
wait for many months while an ordinary house was
built.

When these temporary homes were first put up,
housing officials said that they could only be
allowed to stand for a few years before being taken
down and replaced by proper permanent buildings. But this rule seems to have been forgotten, as
there are still plenty of 'pre-fabs' in 1973, especially
in London. The people who live in them have
mostly grown very fond of them, and would rather
stay in them than move into high modern flats.
Nearly all the pre-fabs have flourishing gardens,
neatly fenced off from each other, and they look
extremely pretty with roses climbing round their
front doors and hollyhocks as high as the roof. I
have drawn one where the tenant has added a little

A simple Victorian dolls' house, probably made at home.

The house decorated with cats at Henfield, in Sussex.

[32] *A 'Pre-Fab'*

wooden porch, just like a real country cottage.

I have never seen a dolls' house pre-fab, but I want to make one before all the real ones disappear and there are none left to copy. If you know of any near where you live it would be interesting to make a dolls' house version; it would be an easy style to copy, as there is only one storey, and any grey-ish paper would do for the walls. Besides being a toy for today, a house like this would become a useful historical record for the future, especially if it was furnished with a good selection of modern gadgets like pop-up toasters and electric mixers.

Sturdy as cardboard dolls' houses are, if you get really interested sooner or later you'll want to build a wooden one. If you don't feel confident enough to tackle the whole job, start off with a wooden box from the wine merchant or the grocer; it will need a thorough sand-papering (very important if it is to look nice) and then dividing into two or four rooms, according to shape and size. A separate piece of wood will be needed for the front, and, if you can get hold of it, a piece of plywood is excellent for this. Decide on what style the house is to be, and remember the front will need to be slightly higher than the box part if you want a parapet. For a sloping roof you will need extra pieces of wood for the roof and the gables, cut out in just the same shapes as the roof pieces for the cardboard houses.

A wooden house can easily have proper see-through glass windows: draw the shapes on first, measuring carefully, and then make the holes with first a drill and then a special saw with a long thin blade. The simplest way to fit the window panes is to have pieces of glass about an inch bigger all round than the holes, and then stick the glass on from behind, using very strong glue. Cover the sharp edges with any firm woven material – carpet binding is ideal – also held with strong glue. Afterwards these fixings can be hidden under some pretty wallpaper.

The bars between the window panes can either

be painted on with gloss paint and a fine brush (not too difficult if you lay the glass over a sheet of paper with the necessary lines drawn on it, and 'trace' them) or made from thin strips of balsa wood or matchsticks glued to the glass. If you want diamond-shaped leaded lights you can stretch thickish fuse wire over the window panes in a criss-cross pattern; do this *before* the pieces of glass are stuck into position behind the front of the house, and fix the ends of the wires with blobs of glue near the outside edges of the glass oblongs where the fixings will be out of sight. When the window is eventually stuck in position the ends of the wires will be securely sandwiched between the wooden front of the house and the glass.

The front and sides of the house can either be papered with special brick or stone paper, like the cardboard houses, or painted. Most timber merchants keep a stock of decorative wooden 'beadings' which can be bought by the foot. The right sort of beading will make door-frames, window surrounds, drip-stones and all sorts of ornamental mouldings, and these finishing touches will make all the difference to your house.

Anything that I've suggested for cardboard houses – pargetting, cat silhouettes, thatch, date stones and all the rest, can be put on a wooden house, provided they agree with the basic style you've chosen. Don't, for instance, paint a black cat frieze round an elegant Georgian brick front, or put a thatched roof on a pre-fab, as these would look quite wrong on either a real house or a dolls' house.

As with the cardboard houses, it saves trouble to paper the inside of the rooms before fixing on the front – or fronts, if you decide on a double opening. When you have finished everything else the front should be attached with small brass hinges and brass screws. A brass hook called a 'side hook' is the best fastening, and was used on many old dolls' houses. These 'side hooks' are sometimes difficult to find, as many hardware shops don't seem to stock them; but if you persevere you should be able to find one in the end.

If you have an experienced carpenter helping you it isn't all that difficult to make a staircase, but you'll need extra space inside the house to fit in a hall and landing if you have stairs. It seems quite all right to 'cheat' a bit over the actual number of stairs, as if you look at old dolls' houses you'll notice there are often only about eight steps between each storey, and they rise very steeply – it would in fact be most difficult for the tiny dolls to climb them, but details like this never seem to matter with toys.

Do look at as many old dolls' houses as you can before you begin anything too ambitious. Getting the right general 'look' is more important than a lot of detail – usually it's far better to keep the building simple, with just a front door and at the most four windows.

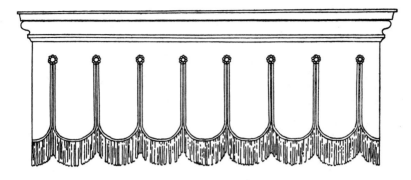

Furnishing
Your
Dolls' House

Dolls' House Furniture

Grown-up collectors are always on the look-out for old dolls' house furniture, and any bits and pieces you see in an antique shop are sure to be too rare and expensive for putting in a toy house. But luckily there is plenty of very good modern dolls' house furniture still being made; it is all mass-produced of course, and lots of it is made of plastic, but this means that it is cheap enough for pocket-money shopping. Many toy shops, for some unknown reason, never seem to stock miniature furniture, though their shelves are always loaded with miniature cars. If you can't find what you want for your house, try asking the shopkeeper if he can get it for you. A firm called A. Barton & Co. Ltd. makes attractive old-fashioned wooden furniture, including four-poster beds, and a series of delightful miniature accessories including a full set of dolls' house ovenware complete with two sizes of casserole and a soufflé dish! Another firm called 'Dol-Toi' makes more wooden furniture and a fascinating assortment of smaller pieces: for a few pence you can get a telephone, an ironing board, a bird cage, a leopard skin rug, a vacuum cleaner and a host of other tiny things – my own favourite is a set of three flying duck ornaments to hang on the sitting room wall, exactly like the ones which were popular for real houses in the 1930s.

Combex's 'Samantha Ann' plastic furniture is made in Hong Kong and is marvellous value – a very small cash outlay will equip a dolls' house with a set of six Chippendale chairs, an extending dining table, and a dear little writing desk with a proper flap and pull-out slides to support it. Lundby is a Swedish firm which exports rather more expensive wooden furniture and all sorts of in-triguing bits and pieces like chandeliers which really work and genuine-looking Persian rugs. Woolworths sometimes have toy furniture, usually in light-coloured plastic suitable for kitchens, bathrooms and nurseries.

Bought furniture is a great help to begin with, but you can make your house more interesting, and have much more fun with it, if you make some of the pieces yourself. Keep a box for storing useful odds and ends, and collect the following things: Cotton reels, corks, cardboard tubes, wood from cigar and date boxes, lollipop sticks, toothpicks and manicure sticks, pipe cleaners, long glass-headed pins and the shorter 'map tacks' with coloured heads, all sorts of beads, stiff backs from writing pads, small pictures from magazines and Christmas cards, lengths of ribbon and thin material, scraps of felt and Fablon, wallpaper, the tops from tubes and jars, artificial flowers, fuse wire. Matchboxes are the most useful of all – if you can find them collect all three sizes, the flat 'Smokers' boxes, the ordinary household sort, and the very small ones usually sold by tobacconists.

A matchbox chest-of-drawers almost makes itself – it's just a matter of sticking six or more boxes together and covering them with brown or any other coloured paper. You can stick four round beads underneath for feet, and push in map tacks or paper fasteners for drawer handles. Experiment with matchboxes as if they were building bricks, putting them together in different ways to make various pieces of furniture – shelves, fireplaces and

so on – and be sure the size is right for your house before doing any glueing. Here are just a few ideas for using matchboxes, but you will be able to think of lots of others for yourselves:

1 Three ordinary matchboxes stuck side-by-side make a single bed. Add four bead feet and a headboard made from a piece of card; the mattress is plastic foam or cotton wool, and the bedclothes are cut from scraps of fine material.

2 The basic chest-of-drawers, without the feet but with a Fablon top, makes a kitchen cabinet. Matchbox trays, without the covers, can be stuck on the wall above the cabinet to make kitchen shelves.

3 Matchbox trays on their own can also be stuck direct to the walls, either singly or in groups, for bookshelves and display cabinets for ornaments.

4 A matchbox standing on its side is the right shape for a television set – it just needs a silver paper screen and a row of knobs drawing on.

5 The same shape does well for a *dolls' house* dolls' house, covered with white paper and then with door and windows added.

6 The smallest size of matchbox is about right for a dolls' house suitcase, covered with brown paper and with a thin strip of brown paper for the handle. Print the doll's initials on the lid, and make a tiny tie-on label with cotton 'strings'.

One of the quickest ways to transform a dolls' house room is to put a folding screen across one corner; you can make the foundation in literally one minute by folding a piece of thick paper or thin card into four equal widths so that it will stand up in a 'W' shape. Victorian scrap screens are very popular again now, and a miniature version is easily made by covering each panel with tiny pictures overlapping each other – use stamps, magazine illustrations and bits cut from gift-wrapping paper. For a true Victorian look, try to find plenty of kittens, pretty little girls, and roses.

Caps from tooth-paste tubes make good flower pots. Stand one on its head, fill it with plasticine and then push in a small artificial flower.

Collect nuts if you live in the country: besides conker furniture, which has already been described, you can have bowls made from acorn cups and a nice little cradle made from three-quarters of a walnut shell. To prevent the cradle tipping backwards I dropped a spot of sealing wax inside the shell about where the baby's feet would be, and this counterbalances the weight of the 'hood'.

Wooden cotton reels can be turned into stools, with little padded cushions on the seats. They are also useful for tubs to stand outside the front door, holding bushes made from fir cones. The fir cones are just glued onto the top of the reel, which should be painted a good bright colour. The top of a face-cream jar stuck on top of another cotton reel becomes a coffee table; it looks very smart with a circular table cloth reaching down to the ground.

You remember those mounted stags' heads in the early nineteenth century dolls' houses? They can't be bought now, of course, but it is quite easy to make them by beheading small plastic animals – stags or buffaloes or anything fierce-looking will do – and then sticking the heads on to shield-shaped pieces of cardboard. Use a very small saw or a sharp knife to cut through the neck.

Anyone who likes sewing can quickly run up some tiny cushions from a length of ribbon, with cotton wool for stuffing; embroidered ribbon is particularly pretty. I have managed to make a pillow and quilt for my walnut shell cradle, and some clever dolls' house owners even do patchwork scaled down to the right size.

Long glass-headed pins pushed through two thin cardboard discs made a pretty birdcage, which can be hung from the ceiling on a length of cotton. For an extra finish, glue a decorative button to the underneath of the cage. Pictures are simplest of all, and as soon as you hang a few up the dolls' house begins to look very real; they can either be stuck straight onto the walls, or mounted on a piece of card and framed with matchsticks painted gold.

Some things which aren't meant for dolls' houses at all fit in very well. For instance, souvenir shops sometimes have tiny brass candlesticks which are absolutely perfect, and they can be fitted with birthday cake candles. Other cake decorations come in useful too – some candle-holders make good ornaments or toys for the nursery; the white fluted pillars intended for wedding cakes are ready-made pedestals for grand drawing rooms, topped with a little statue or a tooth-paste-cap 'vase' of flowers. Broken jewellery, especially odd earrings and metal charms, provides more ornaments. One of my most successful 'finds' is a knight in full armour: he is made of plastic, and came from a souvenir shop. Standing in the dolls' house hall under the mounted stag's head, the plastic knight looks just like a suit of armour in a stately home.

A handbag mirror can be turned into a hanging mirror for a dolls' house wall. I stuck mine onto a piece of card which I had cut out to make a Chippendale-style frame copied from a real one. All sorts of tin lids and bottle caps are useful for trays, dishes and cooking pots: an oblong 'elastoplast' top with a flower picture stuck on made a tea tray, and cooking pots made from bottle caps only need a button 'lid' to complete them.

Toy watches can be converted into clocks. Coloured advertisements for magazines often include miniature reproductions of magazine covers, and if these are carefully cut out they are ideal for dolls' houses. Little oblongs of wood or thick cardboard, suitably covered, look like books. A dolls' house writing table can have tiny sheets of paper on it (just cut them out from a piece of ordinary writing paper) and a canary's feather makes a good quill pen.

Dolls' house kitchens should always be as full as possible. The commercially-made modern food is very good, and so is a lot of the kitchen furniture, refrigerators, cooking stoves and so on. But it is fun to add things like small shells from the seaside which look like scallops or oysters. For that matter what about a minute piece of seaweed hanging up so that the dolls can forecast the weather? Tiny glass jars – the kind chemists put pills in – make containers for rice or sago or hundreds-and-thousands, and the little tin moulds meant for petits-fours are just the right size for dolls' house baking tins.

The more detail you can get *inside* your house the more interesting it will be. The things we remember best from the Victorian dolls' houses are the chess sets, the ivory binoculars, the globes and the cross-stitch pictures saying 'Home Sweet Home'; it is finishing touches like these that make all the difference, and you can never have too many of them. If you're like me, once you begin collecting you'll go on and on.